WAKING UP WITH

THE

RIGHT MINDSET

50 Positive Thoughts to Start Your Day

By

Ivory Joe Hunter, III

Published by Publishing Advantage Group

ISBN: 9781793461087

DEDICATION

This book is dedicated to my three amazing daughters Mariah, Sienna, and Olivia; you girls are my why and I love you to the moon and back. To Kean and Serena, my amazing young adult children through love. To my beautiful mother, Maria, who raised me the right way. To my incredibly talented grandmother, Juanita, who taught me how to dream, and my amazing loving grandmother, Big Mot, who taught me how to love unconditionally. To all of my amazing friends and family who inspire me daily to become a better person. There are too many to name, but you know who you are because I tell you all the time how I feel about you. And finally, this book is dedicated to my dad, Ivory Joe Hunter, Jr., my grandfathers, Ivory Joe Hunter, Sr., Marshall Starks, and Vernal Francis Anderson; may all of you continue to enjoy your transition, I miss you and love you.

ACKNOWLEDGEMENT

The completion of this book could not have been done without the assistance of the many people who have inspired me, supported me and encouraged me along my amazing journey. I am so grateful for you all because in one way or another, you have touched me with experiences that are forever embedded in my heart. There are way too many to name so I'm not going to even attempt to write the list because I don't want to offend anyone. I will, however, make a special acknowledgement to my brothers and sisters, Bobby, Juanee, Erica, Danielle, Jerry, Alvie, Reggie, Mia, and Jeremy. Thank you to my cousin, Chuck, for inspiring me to write this book. I love you all!

With Love,

Ivory

Table of Contents

INTRO:

The beauty of the morning is not in the freshness of the air; it is the freshness of your mind, feelings and thoughts. When we fall asleep, our momentum stops. That basically means that what we experienced before we fell asleep ceases, and we wake up refreshed. It doesn't mean that whatever issue you may have been having just magically vanished or fixed itself while you slept. It simply means that the negative feelings about the situation that you were feeling before you fell asleep stopped. And now what you CHOOSE to FOCUS on when you wake up is totally up to you. Everyday isn't always going to be a good day, but we can choose to try to have the right mindset every day. People are always asking me how and why I always stay so positive, and I always respond that I'm grateful to be alive. Everything starts with gratitude, and it's my choice to have this mindset. It takes daily practice to stay centered and aligned, because there are so many things that happen outside of our control, and we have to work to control our own alignment. So, welcome the new day with a smile on your face, love in your heart, and positive thoughts in your mind. Your mind is a beautiful thing; when you fill it with positive thoughts, your life will start to change. It's not a coincidence that I'm writing a book filled with positive thoughts. I've been reading them for years. I have always made it my intention to better myself, so I've always read positive material, listened to inspirational speakers, and surrounded myself with like-minded individuals. One of my favorite quotes I read was from a book called the Alchemist by Paulo Coehlo is "When we try to become better than who we are, everything around us becomes better." This book will help you become a better you, because it's designed to make you become more self-aware and conscious. I want to share my path to happiness, understanding, and growth with anyone who so graciously reads this book of Thoughts, To-Dos, Take Away's, and a personal 30Day Challenge.

30-Day CHALLENGE- The 30-Day Challenge is your very own personal challenge that you do to better yourself and develop discipline in one or more areas in your life. You decide when to start, and what goals you want to set for yourself. For example, when I did my first 30-Day Challenge, I made it my daily goal to meditate, give up sugar, give up carbs, do 300 push-ups, and 300 sit-ups. It was tough initially, but I started to fall in love with discipline and it became easier and easier. It's totally up to you regarding what goal or goals you choose. Have fun, don't beat yourself up, and remember that consistency unlocks discipline.

When you start, make sure that you:

A.) Write down the day

B.) Write down your goals

C.) Check yes/no for result box

D.) Track your results

1- GIVE LOVE

MORNING THOUGHT

One of the most important things that I have learned in this life is to be a blessing to others. There is joy in giving, and that doesn't always have to mean financially. There are many ways to give; give love. Make a conscious effort today to say hello to everyone you cross paths with. It's truly amazing when you walk around all day and you attract positive encounters with people. Saying hello to someone might be all they need to feel good about themselves. When you put out love, love returns. Mother Theresa said, "It's not how much we give, but how much love we put into giving." Your greatness is not what you have, it's what you give. Have an amazing day.

TO DO: Write down five people in your life and three reasons why you love them. Then, call them today and tell them.

1._____

2._____

3._____

4._____

5._____

TAKE AWAY: Make an effort to put love out there in the universe.

30-Day CHALLENGE

DAY____   GOAL   Result (Y/N)

1._____   _____

2._____   _____

3._____   _____

2- ALIGNMENT FIRST

MORNING THOUGHT

What matters most is your alignment. Being spiritually aligned means discovering the essence of your being and the deepest values by which you live by. You connect to a higher source of intelligence or power, identifying with something greater than the self. Don't force anything into your life. When making decisions, learn to trust your instincts, and if doesn't feel right, don't proceed. Alignment is always first. When you live your life with the mindset of trying to always stay aligned, you become more proactive in your life and less reactive. Your alignment affects your perception of things, people, and circumstances. We can't control the conditions outside of us, so we must practice staying aligned as much as possible in order to be in control of our reactions to potential contrast. In doing so, you will definitely live a more peaceful life. Have an amazing day.

TO DO: Practice Daily Meditation - Follow these steps

1. Sit or lie comfortably
2. Close your eyes
3. Make no effort to control the breath, simply breath naturally
4. Focus your attention on the breath, and how the body moves with each inhalation and exhalation
5. Do this for 5-20 minutes

TAKE AWAY: Control your own alignment because that's really all you can control.

30-Day CHALLENGE

DAY____   GOAL   Result (Y/N)

1._____   _____

2._____   _____

3._____   _____

#3- BE GRATEFUL, & GROW

MORNING THOUGHT

Today is the perfect day to be **Grateful** and **Grow** (2G's). Be grateful that you woke up because some people didn't wake up this morning. Grow by doing something that you have been putting off for one reason or another. Learn something new or practice getting better at something you are already good at. Don't have a "fixed mindset" or a "This is just who I am attitude." Just like the universe expands, so must we, because we are just like the universe. We all have the ability to constantly grow when we don't resist the changes and challenges. We need to know and experience what we don't want in order to know what we do want. Be great today at whatever you do. Keep the 2G mindset and you will always be on the leading edge of life. Have an awesome day!

TO DO: Write a paragraph or two of everyone and everything you're grateful for.

_____

_____

_____

_____

_____

_____

_____

_____

_____

_____

TAKE AWAY: It all starts with gratitude.

30-Day CHALLENGE

DAY____   GOAL   Result (Y/N)

               1._____   _____

               2._____   _____

               3._____   _____

#4- YOU ARE SO DESERVING

MORNING THOUGHT

The better you feel, the more you allow, and you are so DESERVING. Loving yourself starts with liking yourself, which starts with respecting yourself, which starts with thinking of yourself in positive ways. You woke up today, so you can make some type of positive impact in the world today. Just by being you. Don't let anyone tell you that you can't do something, or make you feel unworthy. You are amazing, and so deserving of all of your hearts desires, don't you block desires because of negative beliefs, and don't allow anyone else to block you from your desires because of their negative beliefs. Make a conscious effort to love yourself today. Eat right, work out, and guard your mind from negative thoughts. You were born to be great. Muhammad Ali says, "To be a great champion, you must believe you are the best. If you're not, pretend you are." Have an amazing day!

TO DO: Write "I am so deserving of _____" (You fill in the blank). Write it five times.

1._____

2._____

3._____

4._____

5._____

TAKE AWAY: You deserve your heart's desires and only you can block yourself from them.

30-Day CHALLENGE

DAY____   GOAL   Result (Y/N)

                   1._____   _____

                   2._____   _____

                   3._____   _____

#5- DON'T KILL YOUR IDEAS WITH DOUBT

MORNING THOUGHT

Don't kill your ideas with doubt! If you don't truly believe in whatever it is that you want; you're never going to obtain whatever it is that you're seeking. The law of attraction is a universal law that is a belief that states by focusing on positive or negative thoughts, people can bring positive or negative experiences in their life.

So, don't allow any doubt or negative thoughts to block you from getting what you want.

"You will see it when you believe it," Dr. Wayne Dyer. Don't allow any doubt in at all.

Go get it! Have an amazing day!

TO DO: Write down five goals that you have accomplished this past year just so you can remind yourself how awesome you really are.

1._____

2._____

3._____

4._____

5._____

TAKE AWAY: Don't block your desires with doubt. Learn to focus on the good and allow things to happen.

30-Day CHALLENGE

DAY_____   GOAL   Result (Y/N)

            1._____   _____

            2._____   _____

            3._____   _____

#6- RECOGNIZE RESISTANCE

MORNING THOUGHT

Recognize resistance and learn to LET IT GO. Resistance is the refusal to accept or comply with something, the attempt to prevent something by action or argument. Often, we are trying to force a situation to work out in our favor, but the wise thing to do is just to allow things to unfold naturally. Maybe you have been trying to attract more money, or the love of your life, or a new job, or better health. Either way, change your focus and allow things to come into your life; trying to force things just makes you focus on the absence of it, and keeps you away from what you want. Remember that what we give attention to grows. The universe knows your intentions, so don't fight, just allow things to unfold. Have a beautiful day!

TO DO: Follow these steps.

1. Be honest with yourself about a situation (No self-judgment)
2. Do something today that will make you feel like you accomplished something
3. Focus on something else
4. Look for stories that change your expectations

TAKE AWAY: Don't force things, just allow things to unfold naturally. My grandmother used to always tell me to "let go and let God."

30-Day CHALLENGE

DAY____   GOAL   Result (Y/N)

                    1._____   _____

                    2._____   _____

                    3._____   _____

#7-THIS LIFE IS TEMPORARY

MORNING THOUGHT

This life is temporary but our souls are eternal, so make the most of your human experience. Be the best you that you can be. One of my favorite quotes is, "We are not human beings having spiritual experiences, we are spiritual beings having human experiences." It was by Dr. Wayne Dyer. Once I read this quote, something shifted in me and I lost my fear of death. I realized I had the make the most out of this human experience, and I truly started to live. Tomorrow isn't promised, actually the next moment isn't promised, so be grateful and positive as much as possible. Someone didn't wake up today, but you did! Take advantage of that and be grateful and make the most of your human experience! Have a beautiful day!

TO DO: Do three things you didn't have planned for the day. Be spontaneous and live.

1. Call five people unexpectedly and tell them you love them and are just thinking of them.
2. (Be good to yourself)/ Don't eat or drink anything unhealthy today.
3. Buy a stranger a cup of coffee or feed a homeless person.

TAKE AWAY: Don't take life for granted. Be the best version of you and live fully and lovingly.

30-Day CHALLENGE

DAY____   GOAL   Result (Y/N)

                    1._____   _____

                    2._____   _____

                    3._____   _____

#8- WOMEN ARE ONE OF THE GREATEST CREATIONS

MORNING THOUGHT

Women, I'm just reminding you of just how amazing you are, and how you are one of the greatest creations ever. Gina Carey said, "A strong woman looks at a challenge in the eye and gives it a wink." You are more powerful than you know; you are beautiful just the way you are. .If you are a man reading this, take the time today to acknowledge the females in your life and tell them how amazing they are. A woman who walks with confidence and knows her purpose doesn't have to chase people or opportunities. Her light causes people and opportunities to pursue her. Women, be resilient and unapologetic and make today great. Have an amazing day!

TO DO: Tips to build self-confidence

1. Take ownership of your life
2. Try new things to really experience life
3. Set goals and develop action plan
4. Stick with it
5. Focus yourself into feeling good
6. Get an accountability partner

TAKE AWAY: Women, you are diamonds and they can't break you.

30-Day CHALLENGE

DAY____	GOAL	Result (Y/N)
	1._____	_____
	2._____	_____
	3._____	_____

#9- DON'T DIM YOUR LIGHT

MORNING THOUGHT,

Don't use your time here to serve other people's ego by playing it small. Only you can dim the light which shines from within. You were born with your own unique gifts, feelings, and thoughts to share with others; holding them back is preventing you from experiencing all your hearts desires. One of my favorite singers of all time is Luther Vandross. He started out as a background singer for great artists like Bette Midler, Diana Ross, Barbara Streisand, and the list goes on. Imagine if he spent his career in the background supporting others. The world wouldn't have ever gotten the chance to hear his amazing music. It's definitely a beautiful feeling to help support and encourage others. A candle loses nothing by lighting another candle, but don't blow your candle out in order to light another. There are enough candles in the universe and they all can be lit. Stop dimming your light. It's time to shine! Have a beautiful day!

TO DO: Write down five things that excite you in life, but you know you're holding yourself back. Write "I am great at_____ or write "I feel strong about_____." Then, write it on a separate piece of paper and tape it somewhere where you can see and visualize it every morning.

1._____

2._____

3._____

4._____

5._____

TAKE AWAY: Stars don't care about what people think or say about them; their job is to shine.

30-Day CHALLENGE

DAY____   GOAL   Result (Y/N)

                       1._____   _____

                       2._____   _____

                       3._____   _____

#10- THINK, VISUALIZE, & EXPECT IT-

MORNING THOUGHT

Make sure you are clear with your thoughts, so you can have what you truly want in life. Remember that your thoughts turn into things. Visualizing is a tool to generate a feeling, which is where creation truly begins. The next step is to make sure that you're not adding any resistance into the picture with your own false beliefs. You are a winner, visualize the rewards of success. Take a few minutes to visualize this thing that you want. See it, feel it, believe in it. Make that mental blueprint and begin to focus yourself into feeling good. Your desires are unfolding for you. Have an incredible day!

TO DO: Write down something that you really want, and what you feel like having it, and what you're going to do once you get it.

_____

_____

_____

_____

_____

_____

_____

TAKE AWAY: You can have your heart's desires if you see it and don't block it with false beliefs.

30-Day CHALLENGE

DAY____   GOAL   Result (Y/N)

1._____   _____

2._____   _____

3._____   _____

#11- ALL YOUR POWER IS IN THE NOW

MORNING THOUGHT

Get back to who you really are. You got this! All your power is in the now. Make a choice this morning to be the best version of you. Life is a gift, so you must be present. We were all; put on this planet to co-create. Every person that you run into can be an opportunity for you to have an impactful moment, but often we are consumed with our phones or our thoughts, and we walk right past each other. The universe is always sending signs and opportunities for you, but you must be present. Realize that the present moment is all you ever have. Make the 'now' the foremost focus in your life. Have an amazing day!

TO DO: Focus yourself into feeling good and write down how great you feel right now! Only use your phones if absolutely necessary today, stay present and engage in conversations with people throughout the day.

_____

_____

_____

_____

_____

_____

_____

_____

TAKE AWAY: Stay present and control your thoughts because you don't want to miss opportunities the universe is constantly putting in front of you.

30-Day CHALLENGE

DAY____   GOAL   Result (Y/N)

                           1._____   _____

                           2._____   _____

                           3._____   _____

#12- PROTECT YOUR ENERGY

MORNING THOUGHT

Don't waste your energy engaging with people who aren't conscious. If they have negative thoughts and do negative things, you don't need that type of energy in your life. People inspire you or they drain you ~ pick them wisely. Energy is powerful and infectious, so we have to make sure we guard our energy from energy drainers. A lot of times it's hard to avoid negative people because they are friends and family most of the time. However, you have to be selfish with your energy and not allow people to bring you down. The main way you protect your energy is by controlling your own alignment. So, make sure that you are always working on your alignment, so you're not controlled by outside circumstances. Have a beautiful day and delight yourself with positive encounters.

TO DO: Think about the people in your life who are negative and write down a better way you know that you can handle your encounters with them.

_____

_____

_____

_____

_____

_____

_____

TAKE AWAY: Don't allow people to pour their negative energy on you stay aligned and protect your energy.

30-Day CHALLENGE

DAY____   GOAL   Result (Y/N)

                              1._____   _____

                              2._____   _____

                              3._____   _____

#13-DON'T WORRY BE HAPPY-

MORNING THOUGHT

You can't get to happy over there from unhappy over here, because unhappy over here has your attention. It's impossible to get to a satisfied place from a dissatisfied place. You have to be grateful and find the good in where you are now. If you are unhappy, you're going to continue to attract unhappiness. The thing that keeps you from being where you want to be is the awareness of where you are. Things could be a whole lot worse, but all things are relative. Practice the Law of Relativity by relating your situation to something worse than yours, and you will feel good about where you are. You remember the old song "Don't Worry be Happy." Put that in your iTunes and have an amazing day!

TO DO: Write down five things and five people you love that make you happy and focus on them.

THINGS

1.

2.

3.

4.

5.

PEOPLE

1.

2.

3.

4.

5.

Think about how blessed you are to have these things and people on your list. Someone else is so unfortunate not to be able to have this list. Be grateful.

TAKE AWAY: Find something to be grateful for in your life and focus your energy there because it's impossible to go to a place of satisfaction coming from a place of dissatisfaction.

30-Day CHALLENGE

DAY____   GOAL   Result (Y/N)

                    1._____   _____

                    2._____   _____

                    3._____   _____

#14- YOU ARE NOT A TREE

MORNING THOUGHT

Don't just observe reality, create your own reality. Focus your thoughts on the things that you want. You are not a tree. If you don't like the way your life is, change it. Take control of your life; you can have whatever you want if you would stop blocking your desires with doubt and resistance. A belief is only a thought that you continue to think. Don't be afraid of change because on the other side of those bold steps we take to change our lives, are often the reward. Don't continue to watch the parade go by; jump on in there and live and experience this life the way you were created to. Have an amazing day.

TO DO: Write down three things that you're not happy about in your life and then write down the solution and how you can change them.

NOT HAPPY

1._____

2._____

3._____

SOLUTION

1._____

2._____

3._____

TAKE AWAY: If you don't like your situation, change it. Don't let anything stop you from being happy.

30-Day CHALLENGE

DAY_____   GOAL   Result (Y/N)

1._____   _____

2._____   _____

3._____   _____

#15- THE CORK IS ABOUT TO POP-

MORNING THOUGHT

Stay positive and trust! That cork is about to pop open for you and all your creative ideas will begin flowing. I know you may have some amazing ideas bubbling up inside you that are ready to just explode. It may not seem like it's not happening fast enough, or even at all. Well guess what, it's going to happen. All you have to do is not block your desire with your own false beliefs and doubt. All things are possible, not some. So, don't give up on your dream; focus on smaller dreams that don't seem as "big" or unattainable. The key is to grab the momentum of those "smaller" victories while your "big" dream unfolds. Have a beautiful day!

TO DO: Write down five goals that you have already accomplished this past year. Doesn't matter how big or small.

1.

2.

3.

4.

5.

TAKE AWAY: Just a little reminder of how amazing you are and a reminding you that you can accomplish whatever you want in life!

30-Day CHALLENGE

DAY____	GOAL	Result (Y/N)
	1._____	_____
	2._____	_____
	3._____	_____

#16- STOP COMPLAINING-

MORNING THOUGHT

Don't tell everyone what happened to you, just stay positive, and show them how you handle things when you are aligned. Complaining never makes anything better, it only increases the negative momentum and draws more negative energy and experiences to you. Stephen Hawking says, "people won't have time for you if you are always angry or complaining." Don't be that person or allow people to be constant complainers in your life. Change your energy when you feel like complaining by focusing on something or someone who makes you happy. Besides, whatever it is that you're complaining about is contrast that was created in your life so that you can expand. Have a beautiful day!

TO DO: Write down five adjectives that describe how you feel when people are complaining to you and always angry about something. Then, write down five adjectives that describe how you feel when you don't complain and you just let things go. Which list is better?

COMPLAIN   LET GO

1._____   1._____

2._____   2._____

3._____   3._____

4._____   4._____

5._____   5._____

TAKE AWAY: Complaining doesn't make a situation better; your perspective of the situation makes it better.

30-Day CHALLENGE

DAY_____   GOAL   Result (Y/N)

1._____   _____

2._____   _____

3._____   _____

#17- DON'T CARE WHAT OTHERS THINK-

MORNING THOUGHT

Stop giving a damn about what people think of you. We want so badly for people to get us, but that's such a waste of time. If you care about what other people think, you will always be their prisoner. Free yourself from that nonsense because it's not their life, so what you do is none of their business. People don't know what's best for you; what's right for someone else may be completely wrong for you. Worrying about what others think will keep you from your dreams, and you will be the one dealing with the result in the end. Life is too short so listen to your instincts/intuition/consciousness and do whatever it is that you desire. Have an amazing day!

TO DO: Take these five steps to not care about what others think.

1. Find Your real tribe (People who love and appreciate you unconditionally)
2. Make sure you know what you want and be very clear on your desires
3. Let go of perfection
4. Be vulnerable
5. Be your own number 1 fan (you will never be able to make everyone like you)

TAKE AWAY: Worrying about what other people think will always hold you back.

30-Day CHALLENGE

DAY____   GOAL   Result (Y/N)

                1._____   _____

                2._____   _____

                3._____   _____

#18- LOSE THE FALSE BELIEFS-

MORNING THOUGHT

Stop holding so hard to false beliefs because they are keeping you from your desires. Beliefs are just thoughts that we continue to think, some of those beliefs serve you and some don't. When a belief is blocking you from your desires; you must change your beliefs. Change your point of view on the way you see the false beliefs. Most of the emotional drama in your life is created because we look at and interpret things from the point of view of inner judge or victim. The victim point of view generally comes from a place of low self-esteem and fear. The judgement point of view generally comes from ego, and usually involve criticisms. Both points of view don't serve you; so, get out of your head, lose those false beliefs, and stop holding yourself back. Don't let your false beliefs hold you hostage; free yourself and have an amazing day!

TO DO: Write down three examples of some beliefs that you have that you know haven't be serving you in a positive way. Then, write those same three false beliefs from a different perspective without ego, judgment, or fear.

1._____

_____

2._____

_____

2._____

_____

NEW PERSPECTIVE

1._____

2._____

2._____

TAKE AWAY: Your false beliefs are blocking your desires. Learn to change your point of view on beliefs that don't serve you.

30-Day CHALLENGE

DAY____   GOAL   Result (Y/N)

1._____   _____

2._____   _____

3._____   _____

#19- EVERYTHING STARTS WITH MINDSET-

MORNING THOUGHT

With the right mindset; there's nothing that you can't handle. There's a famous quote that I love by Henry Ford, "Whether you think you can, or you think you can't—you're right." Mindset is the established set of attitudes held by someone. However, the great thing about a mindset is the fact that it's not permanent. You can shift your mindset by making a choice to be the best version of you in all areas of your life. Our experiences are constantly giving us the opportunity to expand and grow. It's just up to us to make that choice to have a strong positive mindset that is flexible and always looking to grow. Everything begins inside your mind. With the right mindset you will succeed in all things. Have a beautiful day!

TO DO: Write down something that you know that you have been stubborn about. Then, look at that topic from a different perspective and write that down as well. Allow yourself a chance to have a GROWTH MINDSET by always changing your perspective.

_____

_____

_____

_____

_____

_____

_____

_____

TAKE AWAY: Don't have a fixed mindset; always be willing to grow.

30-Day CHALLENGE

DAY____   GOAL   Result (Y/N)

1._____   _____

2._____   _____

3._____   _____

#20- SOMETIMES IT'S OKAY TO PROCRASTINATE-

MORNING THOUGHT

"Procrastination is the wisdom to not try to force something that you're not vibrationally ready for," says Esther Hicks. What does that mean? It basically means that you're inner being knows that you're not ready for or aligned up with what you want. When we are not really into what we're doing, and we are doing it just because, it never works out right. So, don't force it. Just put your energy into something that you know that you're ready to handle. In doing so, you will create the right energy you need to have in order to complete anything you want. Have a beautiful day.

TO DO: In a brief paragraph, remember a time when you procrastinated and it worked in your favor. Write it down and then let that experience remind you that everything is always working out for you.

_____

_____

_____

_____

_____

_____

_____

_____

TAKE AWAY: If you know you're not ready for something, don't force it.

30-Day CHALLENGE

DAY____   GOAL   Result (Y/N)

                 1._____   _____

                 2._____   _____

                 3._____   _____

#21-STAY FOCUSED-

MORNING THOUGHT

Focusing your energy and thoughts on the reality you desire takes your mind off the reality you're currently in. The key is to place your focus on the outcome and not the obstacles. The Law of Attraction is very real, and we can have whatever it is we desire. It takes consistent daily practice to learn how to control your thoughts and focus on the good. Ask yourself if what you're doing today is getting you closer to where you want to be tomorrow. Abraham Hicks says to "Keep your focus on how you want to feel and let the universe fill in the details. It's really easy to get distracted but remember that your focus determines your reality. Have a beautiful day!

TO DO: – Write a list of five things that you want to accomplish today and focus your energy on getting them done today.

1.

2.

3.

4.

5.

TAKE AWAY: You can have anything your heart desires when you have focused positive energy.

30-Day CHALLENGE

DAY____   GOAL   Result (Y/N)

                 1._____   _____

                 2._____   _____

                 3._____   _____

#22- YOU ARE MORE THAN A CONQUEROR

MORNING THOUGHT

Today is absolutely the day for you to know that you are incredible. There isn't anything that can stand in your way with the right mindset. Romans 8:37 says "In all things we are more than conquerors." Notice that it didn't say some things, it said all things. Mahatma Gandhi says, "Freedom is not worth having if it does not include the freedom to make mistakes." So be fearless in all you do, because there is no such thing as failure, only learning experiences. Oprah Winfrey was born into poverty in Mississippi but that didn't stop her from going on to becoming the richest African- American of the 20th century. So, don't let anything or anyone stop you from doing whatever your heart desires. Lose those false beliefs and have an amazing day!

TO DO: Try these six steps.

1. Identify your resistance
2. Break your goals into smaller pieces
3. Talk to someone who accomplished a similar goal
4. Put your plan in writing
5. Track your progress
6. Visualize your goal for inspiration

TAKE AWAY: Only thing holding you back is you there's nothing that you can't overcome with the right mindset. No FEAR!

30-Day CHALLENGE

DAY____   GOAL   Result (Y/N)

1._____   _____

2._____   _____

3._____   _____

#23- MAKE PEACE WITH WHERE YOU ARE

MORNING THOUGHT

Making peace with where we are always moves us in the direction of where we want to go. You are where you are for a reason, so don't fight it, embrace it and stay present, and you will get the lesson. There isn't any judgment in that, so stop beating yourself up. Whatever is going on in your life will definitely pass because there is nothing permanent in life. Remember that you are right where you're supposed to be, to get what you're supposed to get, and go where you're destined to be. I remember a time when I was very disappointed because I broke my foot. It was so upsetting because I had a great routine going in order to get back in shape, and I knew I wasn't going to be able to exercise or drive anymore for a few months. Talk about crushed; I was torn. The universe sat my butt down but, luckily, I got over it and embraced it because it was during that time of stillness that I got the inspiration to work on a life changing project. If I wouldn't have gotten hurt, I would've continued with the same daily routine running around, and the project would have never manifested. So, stay present and positive, and embrace where you are. Have an amazing day.

TO DO: Take several minutes to think about your current situation and then write down how you can see the positive aspects of being where you are.

_____

_____

_____

_____

_____

_____

_____

_____

TAKE AWAY: You are where you are for a reason, embrace it and make peace with it. You're still headed toward your destiny!

30-Day CHALLENGE

DAY____   GOAL   Result (Y/N)

1._____   _____

2._____   _____

3._____   _____

#24- ATTITUDE OF GRATITUDE

MORNING THOUGHT

Having an attitude of gratitude is always a great place to start from. We have to be satisfied with what is and eager for more. If you want to be happy, find gratitude in something or someone. When we are ungrateful and unhappy, we block good things from happening to us. Someone else is in a far worse situation than you and wish they had your problems. Not to say what you're experiencing isn't difficult to deal with, but it could be a whole lot worse. You woke up today and you're reading this. That is a blessing in itself because there are so many people who didn't wake up today. Gratitude unlocks your blessings, resistance blocks your blessings. It is not happy people who are thankful, it is thankful people who are happy. Have a great day.

TO DO: Write down three things you're grateful for. Write down three people you couldn't live without.

THINGS

    1._____

    2._____

    3._____

PEOPLE

    1._____

    2._____

    3._____

TAKE AWAY: Be grateful; things could be a lot worse. You are blessed!

30-Day CHALLENGE

DAY____   GOAL   Result (Y/N)

                    1._____   _____

                    2._____   _____

                    3._____   _____

#25- BE DRIVEN

MORNING THOUGHT

Motivation and inspiration are temporary feelings you get when you want to attempt to accomplish something, but those feelings come and go. Being driven is a mindset that doesn't change because it's a part of your lifestyle and who you are. When you are driven you can accomplish anything at any time. If you're not driven, you can't cultivate your talent because once you rest and get comfortable, your talent and desires start to diminish. So, make up your mind today to shift the way you have been approaching things. A driven individual is always going to be consistent and relentless in their pursuits. You are amazing! Have a powerful, lovely day!

TO DO: Focus on these seven steps to become self-driven

1. Believe in yourself

2. Challenge yourself

3. Learn and continue learning

4. Invest into personal development

5. Meet more people

6. Use failure as a motivator to do your best

7. Never stop; never settle

TAKE AWAY: With a driven mindset, you can accomplish whatever you want.

30-Day CHALLENGE

DAY____   GOAL   Result (Y/N)

1._____   _____

2._____   _____

3._____   _____

#26- LET GO OF YESTERDAY

MORNING THOUGHT

Let go of yesterday and enjoy today. Everything is working out for YOU! My little brother Bobby wrote a song years ago and one of the lines from the song was "Yesterday is gone, Tomorrow's not promised, so focus on today. The universe is constantly sending you signs in so many different ways. If you are consumed with things that happened yesterday, you are potentially missing out on amazing opportunities today. So, focus on today; you have such an amazing gift that you need to share with someone today, or someone needs to share their amazing gift with you. Either way you have to be present in order for that to happen. Have a beautiful day of positive impact and love.

TO DO: Write a "to-do" list for the day. Write down 5 things you need to do that you may have been putting off, and make sure you focus and get them done. (For example: Pay a bill, call someone, clean out your closet and donate clothes to goodwill, cook a special meal).

1._____

2._____

3._____

4._____

5._____

TAKE AWAY: "Yesterday is gone. Tomorrow has not yet come. We only have today. Let us begin." - Mother Teresa

30-Day CHALLENGE

DAY____   GOAL   Result (Y/N)

                        1._____   _____

                        2._____   _____

                        3._____   _____

#27- BE CONCIOUS OF YOUR THOUGHTS

MORNING THOUGHT

Be conscious of your thoughts and the right actions will always be there. Through your mind you create your reality, because thoughts become things. Your thoughts become words, and your words become your behavior, your behavior becomes your habits, your habits become your values, and your values become your destiny. As you see it all, starts with your thoughts so be mindful of what you're thinking about, and when it's not a thought that is serving you, let it go and think of a more positive thought. Have an incredible day!

TO DO: Try practicing these exercises today.

1. Only use positive words when talking today
2. Fill your mind with positive thoughts
3. Smile all day
4. Make Peace with the past
5. Be grateful
6. Use the "mirror technique" whenever you walk past a mirror say something positive about yourself

TAKE AWAY: Once you become consciously aware of just how powerful your thoughts are, you will start to understand that everything in your life is exactly how you allow it to be.

30-Day CHALLENGE

DAY____   GOAL   Result (Y/N)

             1._____   _____

             2._____   _____

             3._____   _____

#28- STOP & ALIGN

MORNING THOUGHT

When you feel anxiety and want to work harder to try to fix a situation, that's the sign to stop and align yourself, because you're not in sync with your inner being. Remember that it's impossible to go to a place of satisfaction from a place of dissatisfaction because dissatisfied has your attention. Take the time to center yourself first. In fact, take all of the time that you need because your alignment comes first, and it's really the only thing that you can control. If you keep the energy of anxiety, you will continue to attract more of the thing that's causing you the contrast. When you are in full alignment with the source within you, you're not reactive to the contrast going on around you. As opposed to being sucked into the contrast happening around you, you're influenced by your alignment with the source within you. So, let it go, and tune yourself into a better feeling because all is well and you are safe in the universe. Have a beautiful day of clarity!

TO DO: Practice these three steps to align yourself.

1. Do something that makes you feel good
2. Meditate
3. Repeat step 1

TAKE AWAY: It is never a good idea to try to fix a problem when your energy is off; take the time to align yourself.

30-Day CHALLENGE

DAY____	GOAL	Result (Y/N)
	1._____	_____
	2._____	_____
	3._____	_____

#29- ENVIRONMENT MATTERS

MORNING THOUGHT

It's been said that the five people closest to you shape your success, your interests, and much more about you than you even realize. If that is truly the case, we need to be very selective of our friends and the company we keep. Energy is so infectious so you need to protect your energy and try your best to keep positive people in your life who challenge you to become better. It's about having a growth mindset; challenge yourself. A lot of people get used to being comfortable and settle when we are meant to live abundantly in so many ways. I left my small amazing hometown of Bristol, Pa when I was 20 years old. Sure, I was one of the big fish in a small pond but I wanted more. I moved to California where I would become a small fish in a big pond. I'm grateful for that move because being a small fish in a big pond keeps me with the growth mindset. There's nothing wrong with either, because I love the people I grew up with but understand that your environment is constantly shaping you. So be very conscious of where you live, where you work, and who you spend your time with. Create the environment that you desire in all areas of your life. Have a beautiful day!

TO DO: Think about the five people closest to you that you spend your time with. Are they making you better or are they draining you and keeping you stuck? Think about your job. Are you happy there? Are you happy with the people you work with? Where do you live? Are you happy where you live? Are you happy with the people you live with? Are you happy with you neighbors? Think about all of this and if you're not satisfied with any of it; make sure you change it.

TAKE AWAY: Your environment is shaping you; create the environment you want for yourself in order to continuously grow.

30-Day CHALLENGE

DAY____   GOAL   Result (Y/N)

1._____   _____

2._____   _____

3._____   _____

#30- HOLD YOUR INTENTIONS TO YOURSELF

MORNING THOUGHT

When we hold our intentions to ourselves, they can be more powerful. Remember that everybody that we are speaking to about our ideas and thoughts aren't always happy for us. They can be energy blockers, sometimes intentionally and sometimes unintentionally. Their lack of belief can affect your belief, and you definitely don't want anyone else's doubt to stop you from achieving the things you desire. I understand the feeling of wanting to be validated to feel better about your intentions. I also understand how you may be telling others your plans to motivate yourself. However, tests have been done since 1933 that show people who talk about their intentions are less likely to make them happen. You have nothing to prove; do whatever you're doing because you are inspired by the source inside you to do so. Have an amazing day!

TO DO: Follow these FIVE steps for powerful intentions:

1. Meditate
2. Release your intentions and desires
3. Be content where you are
4. Detach from the outcome
5. Let the universe handle the details

TAKE AWAY: Keep it a secret! Shhhhhh...

30-Day CHALLENGE

DAY____   GOAL   Result (Y/N)

              1._____   _____

              2._____   _____

              3._____   _____

#31- BE LESS REACTIVE

MORNING THOUGHT

Be less reactive to the conditions around you, and more responsive to the source within you. Reactive people let their circumstances and conditions control them. We can't control what people are going to say to us, or how they may treat us at any given moment. Therefore, we must be proactive in our mindset. That's why it's important to make sure that you are constantly aware of how you are feeling. It's important to practice the art of feeling good because when you feel good, you are in connection with source, and you are aligned. So, when situations occur you're able to see it from the sources perspective, and that's never negative. Have an incredible day!

TO DO: Work on these steps to be less reactive.

1. Take a deep breath. (If you feel angry and upset with someone)

2. Change your point of view (If you're upset, look at it from a different perspective)

3. Or simply walk away

TAKE AWAY: Reactive people are driven by feelings, by circumstances, by conditions, by their environment. Proactive people are driven by values carefully thought about and internalized.

30-Day CHALLENGE

DAY____   GOAL   Result (Y/N)

1._____   _____

2._____   _____

3._____   _____

#32- YOU ARE YOUR BRAND

MORNING THOUGHT

Be excellent and work to create and protect your brand. You are your brand! Yes, you are a brand; everything you do and say is a representation of who you are to the world. So, how are you representing your brand today? I read something somewhere a while ago that said that your smile is your logo. Your personality is your business card. How you leave others feeling after an interaction becomes your trademark. There are 3 elements of your brand that you need to work on daily, and they are physical, mental, and spiritual. Always work on maintaining, growing, and enhancing those parts of your brand and you will have a more fruitful life. Have a beautiful day!

TO DO:

1. Smile (Work on your logo)
2. Have an amazing attitude (Hand out business cards)
3. Make people's day (Create your trademark)

TAKE AWAY: How you look + How you speak + How you act = Your Personal Brand

30-Day CHALLENGE

DAY____   GOAL   Result (Y/N)

1._____   _____

2._____   _____

3._____   _____

#33- DON'T SPLIT YOUR ENERGY

MORNING THOUGHT

Our desires open the door, but our negative beliefs close the door. Don't split your energy; focus on the desires that opened the door. Split energy is when your thoughts, beliefs, feelings (both conscious and subconscious) and actions are not all on the same page. For example, you can't consciously say that you want to find the love of your life and be in a great relationship, when subconsciously you have trust issues and a fear of getting hurt. The Law of Attraction is responding to your subconscious feelings, not what you're saying. In relationships, some people keep attracting partners who cheat because that's what they're subconscious is giving attention to. So, make sure you focus to clean up those subconscious negative beliefs. You deserve to be free of fear. Have a beautiful day!

TO DO:

Step 1. Identify your split energy and write down what you want, and also write down what your resistance or fear is about the thing you desire.

Step 2. Then write down how it feels to have things you desire.

Step 3. Find the feeling of having that thing you desire and focus on the feeling.

TAKE AWAY: Split energy is the best way to sabotage your desires.

30-Day CHALLENGE

DAY_____   GOAL   Result (Y/N)

1._____ _____

2._____ _____

3._____ _____

#34- CONSISTENCY UNLOCKS DISCIPLINE

MORNING THOUGHT

Most people struggle with discipline and view it as some unattainable goal that they are forever trying to reach. However, I have learned through failing forward hundreds of times for years and years that it's not that difficult. Although it's not something you're born with, it's definitely something very attainable and rewarding. It just takes a shift in your mindset and a desire to be disciplined. The key is consistency; you have to train yourself to be consistent. Once you start doing the small things consistently, you create a momentum of positivity while building confidence, and it makes it easier for you to practice discipline in all of your areas of your life. If I can do it, you can do it because I was the worst when it came to discipline. I just decided to change my story and tell the story I wanted to tell. Change your story, you got this. Have an incredible day.

TO DO: How to become disciplined

1. Set goals/Start small/Write them down (Make a daily visual reminder)
2. Know your weaknesses
3. Remove temptation
4. Check off your goals daily to gain confidence

TAKE AWAY: Consistent action creates discipline.

30-Day CHALLENGE

DAY____   GOAL   Result (Y/N)

1._____   _____

2._____   _____

3._____   _____

#35- LET GO OF THE SAW

MORNING THOUGHT

Let go of the (SAW) stress, anxiety, and worry. Do an evaluation of your life. How many times have you been stressing or worrying about something, and it worked out? I'll wait.... Exactly my friend; so, relax and know things are unfolding for you exactly the way they should. The more you focus on the subject that's worrying you or bothering you, the more it's going to grow. You must activate a new thought and take your mind off the subject. And since you're off that subject, you might as well make your new thoughts extremely good thoughts that make you happy. In doing so, you will raise your vibration and allow things to work out. A year from now you'll laugh at whatever's stressing you out today. So why not laugh today? Have an amazing day!

TO DO: When you feel stressed, worried, or anxious try this:

1. Change topic
2. Allow
3. Ignore reality
4. Focus yourself into feeling good (Do things you love to do, talk or spend time with someone who loves you, etc.)

TAKE AWAY: When you have negative thoughts, let them go and focus on new positive thoughts.

30-Day CHALLENGE

DAY____   GOAL   Result (Y/N)

1._____   _____

2._____   _____

3._____   _____

#36- DO LESS ACTION WORK

MORNING THOUGHT

Some days it's better to do less action work and do more vibrational work. As described by Cassandra Sturdy, "Your 'vibration' is a fancy way of describing your overall state of being. Everything in the universe is made up of energy vibrating at different frequencies. Even things that look solid are made up of vibrational energy fields at the quantum level. This includes you. "When your vibration is high, things are flowing for you and you put out amazing energy that attracts people and things to you. When your vibration is low, you don't feel so great, and things don't flow as smoothly for you. With that in mind, focus on raising your vibration today. Have an awesome day.

TO DO: Suggestions to raise your vibration

1. Be conscious of your thoughts
2. Call and have a minimum of three phone calls with people you love
3. Meditate (clear your thoughts and be refresh them)
4. Drink lots of water (Flush out toxicity in your body)
5. Treat your body to some kind of workout
6. Do something nice for someone else
7. Be grateful
8. Listen to some of your favorite music

TAKE AWAY: Your vibration attracts your experiences. Spend time raising your vibration.

30-Day CHALLENGE

DAY____   GOAL   Result (Y/N)

                        1._____   _____

                        2._____   _____

                        3._____   _____

#37- PLANT A HAPPY SEED

MORNING THOUGHT

Being happy is a very personal thing and has nothing to do with anyone else. It is a choice on how we choose to feel, because happiness is an inside job. Don't rely on situations and circumstances to determine your happiness. Instead, plant a happy seed this morning and allow that energy and momentum to give you happy experiences today. We all have heard the old saying, that you reap what you sow. Well it's definitely true that just making a choice to be happy shifts your vibration and starts that energy of positivity flowing your way. Have an amazing day!

TO DO: Take these steps to crank up the happiness (Add your own steps that make you happy)

1. Write down three positive things
2. Listen to your favorite music
3. Make someone's day by texting something loving to them out of the blue
4. Let something go from the past
5. Make plans to do something fun
6. Smile
7. Think positive
8. Straighten out your posture and feel good about yourself

TAKE AWAY: Wake up and think happy thoughts and do things that make yourself and others happy.

30-Day CHALLENGE

DAY____   GOAL   Result (Y/N)

                    1._____   _____

                    2._____   _____

                    3._____   _____

#38- MOVE PAST THE ANGER

MORNING THOUGHT

Move past the anger because the source inside you doesn't feel the same way about the situation or person as you do. Stop that momentum immediately. It is blocking you and holding you back from positive experiences. Anger can cause issues to us emotionally and physically as well as to the people in our lives. Forgiveness of self and forgiveness of others is so important to live a healthy life. When something happens, and someone does something that offends me, I think about the times I offended others, and I work to let it go. I know when I made mistakes that affected others, I wanted forgiveness. It doesn't feel good having someone angry at you. Forgive and forget because you free yourself from the feelings of the negative experience. Have such an amazing day!

TO DO: Forgive someone who you have been holding some resentment or anger towards. (Call/text and say, "I forgive you and truly wish you well.") Or let go of some resentment or regret you have been holding onto. Write it down and then release it. Let it go and free yourself. When you feel up to it, call that person and forgive them.

TAKE AWAY: Buddha says that "Holding on to anger is like grasping a hot coal with the intent at throwing at someone else, you are the one that gets burned."

30-Day CHALLENGE

DAY____	GOAL	Result (Y/N)
	1._____	_____
	2._____	_____
	3._____	_____

#39- IGNORE REALITY

MORNING THOUGHT

Stop using what you want and don't have as an excuse not to feel good. Ignore that and focus on feeling good. To create change, you must not accept the things you don't desire. Looking at your current reality as fact will keep you where you don't want to be. Right before I began writing this book, I received some news that affected my then current reality in a major way. It was something out of my control, yet it was very detrimental to me. I refused to accept it, because I knew that things always work out; I knew that it was important for me to focus on feeling good, and I knew that I had to find the feeling of having my hearts desires without actually physically having them. I knew I had to keep my energy, positive and receptive. If I paid attention to my then current reality, I wouldn't have been present, and this book wouldn't have been thought of. Create the reality you want in your mind and heart. Have an awesome day full of positive impact!

TO DO: If there is something that is affecting your current reality in a negative way, do the following:

1. Ignore it
2. Focus your energy on other things and people
3. Focus on what you want
4. Know that things are working out for you

TAKE AWAY: When you don't like your current reality is, ignore it and focus on the things you want.

30-Day CHALLENGE

DAY____   GOAL   Result (Y/N)

1._____   _____

2._____   _____

3._____   _____

#40- FAIL FORWARD

MORNING THOUGHT

Fail early, fail often, but always fail forward. Failure is merely a price we pay for success. Never be afraid to fail, because when you fail it means two very important things. First, you are brave, because you have to try in order to fail. Secondly, every time you fail there is an opportunity to learn and expand. We are all a part of the universe and just the universe is constantly expanding, so are we. So, don't sit there all nice and cozy in your comfort zone, get outside of comfort and try something new. I love when President Barack Obama said, "The real test is not whether you avoid failure, because you won't. It's whether you let it harden or shame you into inaction, or whether you learn from it." Have a beautiful day!

TO DO: Reflect, Plan, and Do. Write down a time when you failed at something, but it made you better because you attempted it. Then, write down something you have been wanting to try, but for whatever reason you have been afraid to fail. Then set a date and time you're going to do it.

WHAT YOU FAILED AT-

_____

_____

WHAT YOU'RE GOING TO DO-

_____

_____

WHEN-

_____

TAKE AWAY: Failing forward is the ability to get back up after you've been knocked down, learn from your mistake, and move forward in a better direction." – John C. Maxwell

30-Day CHALLENGE

DAY____   GOAL   Result (Y/N)

1._____   _____

2._____   _____

3._____   _____

#41- BE KIND TO THE HOMELESS

MORNING THOUGHT

Some homeless people just want to be acknowledged; it's not always about the money. A simple hello is an act of kindness that can go a long way for them. The homeless epidemic is growing expeditiously out of control, and it's very sad to witness. I know it can get a little overwhelming when we see people living in the streets, but no matter what, we can't afford to ignore them. Empathy and compassion are so underrated; be that person who sets an example on how to treat people less fortunate. Even if it's saying hello and sparking up a conversation that gesture goes along way. Have a beautiful day and make someone else's day!

TO DO: Do the following:

1. Give away your old clothes to the homeless
2. Give away extra blankets you may have to the homeless
3. Get your friends, family, and social network involved (People will help; it just takes "you" to lead the way)

TAKE AWAY: Always be kind and thoughtful to homeless people, that's all some of them may need.

30-Day CHALLENGE

DAY____   GOAL   Result (Y/N)

            1._____   _____

            2._____   _____

            3._____   _____

#42- BECOME POWERFUL

MORNING THOUGHT

Let go of what hasn't been working. Make up your mind to become powerful. Remember that we create our own realities. It's important to control your own alignment and have no fear. You don't have a lot of time to live half-ass or half-fulfilled. You were born into this physical time space reality in order to have impact, so be powerful. It all starts in your mind; make that choice today because you are amazing. Strength isn't obtained from what you accomplish; strength comes from overcoming the things that you thought you couldn't. Educate yourself and do things to become a better you, so you're confident in all you do. Have an incredible day of positive impact!

TO DO: Try doing these things to become powerful

1. Spend time alone working on yourself and your craft

2. Be very clear on the things you want

3. Keep your mind and body healthy

4. Don't waste time (don't spend a lot of time doing things with no benefit)

5. Be a risk taker

6. Surround yourself with powerful-minded people

7. Meditate

TAKE AWAY: "All your power is in your awareness of that power." - Rhonda Byrne's The Secret

30-Day CHALLENGE

DAY____   GOAL   Result (Y/N)

1._____   _____

2._____   _____

3._____   _____

#43- LIVE ABUNDANT

MORNING THOUGHT

Abundance is the ability to do what you need to do, when you need to do it. When most people hear the word abundance, they automatically think of wealth. However, abundance comes in many forms. One can be abundant in love, abundant in appreciation and gratitude, abundant in ideas, abundant in clarity, abundant in money, and, etc. You get the point; the important thing is to share your abundance with others. It feels amazing to give, and it puts out loving energy in the universe. I love one of the many quotes that Abraham Hicks says about abundance. She says, "Like the air you breathe, abundance in all things is available to you. Your life will simply be as good as you allow it to be." Have a beautiful day!

TO DO: Boost up your Confidence today.

1. Smile

2. Prepare yourself for opportunities

3. Have an abundant mentality

4. Be grateful

5. Enjoy life

TAKE AWAY: You were born to live an abundant life

30-Day CHALLENGE

DAY____   GOAL   Result (Y/N)

1._____   _____

2._____   _____

3._____   _____

#44 - *YOUR LOVED ONES NEVER LEAVE YOU*

MORNING THOUGHT

It is totally understandable why most people fear death and dread losing their loved ones. The hardest part of losing someone close to you is learning to live without them. The key is to understand that death is not the end; it is really a transition into the next life. I've learned that life and death are just mere illusions, and we are in a constant state of transformation. Norman Cousins stated that "death is not the greatest loss in life. The greatest loss in life is what dies inside us while we live." Our loved ones who transitioned may not be here with us physically, but they are still here. My father transitioned when he was 44 years old. I was 25 at the time, and I felt like my world was over. However, that's where a new beginning started for me. I had to make sure that I continued to live and became the best version of myself as possible. My father's birthday was July 27, 1951 and I see his number 727 every single day. He, as well as other important people in my life who transitioned, are constantly showing themselves to me. I feel their presence and I see the signs that they give me. Your loved ones are with you as well, just make sure that you are present and aware of their presence. They haven't forgotten about you. You have angels and they want you to live abundantly. Have a beautiful day.

TO DO: Tips to stay connected with your loved ones who transitioned

1. Communicate with them (have conversations out loud with them when you're by yourself)
2. Get rid of false beliefs about being unable to contact the departed
3. Look for signs that they are giving you (numbers of important dates, your dreams, feeling their touch, unexpected electrical activity, their voice, and,
4. etc.)
5. Meditate (put yourself in the receptive mode)

TAKE AWAY: Your loved ones who passed are still with you.

30-Day CHALLENGE

DAY_____   GOAL   Result (Y/N)

1._____   _____

2._____   _____

3._____   _____

#45- PASSION NEVER FAILS

MORNING THOUGHT

It's been said that when you follow your passion, success will follow you. You have to be so good that people can't take their eyes off of you. Today is a day that you never lived before, so be passionate about the day. Don't just go through the motions and settle, look inside your greatness and push yourself to be the best version of you possible. If you're not feeling great about what you're doing, it's not the right path for you. You have to really discover what makes your soul burn with joy and desire to be the best. Be so passionate that you inspire others to want to find their passion. Passion is what makes the world go 'round, love just makes it a safer place. Have an incredible day!

TO DO: Work on your passion today.

1. Know yourself

2. Do your impossible

3. Surround yourself with passionate people

4. Do something that's going to make an impact

TAKE AWAY: The secret ingredient to life is passion.

30-Day CHALLENGE

DAY_____   GOAL   Result (Y/N)

                        1._____   _____

                        2._____   _____

                        3._____   _____

#46- IT'S NEVER TOO LATE

MORNING THOUGHT

Is there some dream you been holding in your heart that you never tried? Are you wanting to go back to school? Get back in shape? Meet the love of your life? Whatever it is, it's not too late. You woke up today so it's definitely possible. Your thoughts can always become things as long as you don't block them with false beliefs that aren't serving you. The famous actor, Morgan Freeman, really didn't get discovered and make it big until he was 52 years old. You can still do whatever you want to do in life; don't let heartaches and failure impede on your growth. They are only meant to challenge you, not stop you. It's never too late, and you're never too old to become better. Joyce Meyer says, "It's never too late for a new beginning in your life." Have an amazing day and go for it!

TO DO: Here's your plan to start something new

1. Identify your desire
2. Set a deadline for when you are going to start
3. Meditate and align yourself up with your desires (Picture the feeling of accomplishing your desires)
4. Do the work (Take all the steps)
5. Have fun

TAKE AWAY: It's never too late to change your life.

30-Day CHALLENGE

DAY____   GOAL   Result (Y/N)

1._____   _____

2._____   _____

3._____   _____

#47- CHANGE YOUR PERSPECTIVE

MORNING THOUGHT

When you change your perspective, it means that you are changing the way you look at things. Being able to have a positive mindset allows you to always look at things from a different perspective. Abraham Hicks uses the phrase "change your point of attraction," which is essentially the same thing. I like the term "change your point of attraction a lot," because it makes you look at what you're pointing at or about a person or situation. I'm always aware of my point attraction when I deal with people. It is my goal to see people the way source sees people. Source looks beyond actions, and truly sees their brokenness, insecurities, resentment, pain and, etc. When people are being mean or rude towards you, it usually never is about you, so don't take it personal. Having this mindset is healthier for you because you don't take on the negative energy. Furthermore, when you are smiling and seeing the good in people, you usually attract that energy from them. So, work on changing the way you look at things and have a beautiful day!

TO DO: Ways you can Change Your Perspective

1. Assume the best of people
2. Stop dreading things; find something to be grateful for about the task
3. Be present and conscious throughout the day
4. Work on losing your judgments about people
5. Growth mindset (Don't be set in your ways)

TAKE AWAY: Changing your perspective, changes your experiences.

30-Day CHALLENGE

DAY____   GOAL   Result (Y/N)

                  1._____   _____

                  2._____   _____

                  3._____   _____

#48- REACH OUT TO LOVED ONES

MORNING THOUGHT

The way things are happening in the world today, is an important reminder to never take the people you love for granted. Say the things that you've been meaning to say. Tomorrow isn't promised to any of us, so reach out to your loved ones today. It could be rather frightening to know that when you see your loved ones, seeing them or talking to them again isn't guaranteed. So, treat people that way when you greet them; tell your loved ones that you love them. It's so easy to get caught up in our own busy lives and lose contact with people who mean so much to us. It has become the norm to just accept that life keeps us busy, consequently we don't make an effort to stay in touch. Don't let that be you; reach out and call that special someone. Have a beautiful day!

TO DO: Make a Top Ten Lists every month of people you have to reach out to. Put it somewhere that you see it often enough to be reminded of your loved ones. Here is your first month.

MONTH_____

1._____   2. _____

3._____   4. _____

5._____   6. _____

7._____   8. _____

9._____   10. _____

TAKE AWAY: Tomorrow is never promised, so love and appreciate the people who are in your life.

30-Day CHALLENGE

DAY____   GOAL   Result (Y/N)

1._____   _____

2._____   _____

3._____   _____

#49- LOSE REGRET

MORNING THOUGHT

Regret is such a waste of moment in time, because in regret you set yourself apart from your inner being who loves you and sees the value in you. Oprah Winfrey says to, "Step out of the history that is holding you back. Step into the new story you are willing to create." Our stories are already written, and we are here to experience and co-create along the journey. I remember I had the most amazing woman, she was the love of my life. She was my dream girl, and I felt like nothing could make me happier than her love. Then we broke up, and I was crushed. I didn't fight it; I let her go. I honestly can say that I have no regrets at all from losing her. I'm grateful for the love we shared because she was incredible, and I'm grateful for that chapter of my life. However, if we didn't end that chapter of our lives, I wouldn't have my amazing daughters in my life who I had after we ended. They are truly the unconditional eternal loves of my life. If I would have resisted and sat around with regrets; I wouldn't have moved on and been available in order to have my daughters. So, trust and know that everything happens for a reason; lose the regrets and stay present. Have an amazing day!

TO DO: Some Tips on How to Let Go of Regrets

1. Be proactive (Don't allow regrets in; be mindful of your decisions)
2. Identify regret (Change point of attraction on situation/see positive)
3. Accept it as a clarifying moment for you
4. Forgive yourself and forgive others
5. Replace thoughts when negative thoughts come
6. Find the good in where you are now!

TAKE AWAY: Regrets become painful burdens that disturb your present happiness. Let them go.

30-Day CHALLENGE

DAY____   GOAL   Result (Y/N)

1._____   _____

2._____   _____

3._____   _____

#50- EMBRACE CONTRAST

MORNING THOUGHT

Always appreciate the opportunity for expansion, because all the contrast you deal with is causing you to expand and grow. Don't fight the experience; embrace it and grow with it. Contrast is an opportunity to focus more clearly on what you truly want. Resistance is the only thing that can slow your expansion and growth. Oprah Winfrey says, "Change your wounds into wisdom." For life to expand, there must be contrast. That's what we came for. Plus, how do you know what you want without knowing what you don't want? Problems are the path to solutions. Contrast is the gap between what you currently have and what you desire. Contrast heightens your desire. It assists you in getting clear about what you need to do, and what actions you need to take. Contrast is essential for you to keep moving forward. Have an amazing day!

TO DO: Use these tips as "Go-to Thoughts" when dealing with contrast.

1. Stop, Cancel, Clear; there's nothing to fear (You are going to be fine)
2. Breathe, trust, and surrender
3. Change Your perspective and look for the good
4. Let go, and let God (There is something greater inside you that's already working things out)
5. Accepting that you created the contrast in order to grow gives you the power to deal with it.

TAKE AWAY: Contrasting moments always brings you clarity when you embrace the experience.

30-Day CHALLENGE

DAY____   GOAL   Result (Y/N)

                    1._____   _____

                    2._____   _____

                    3._____   _____

ABOUT THE AUTHOR

Ivory Hunter is a very creative entrepreneur with a passion for writing and creating positive materials on different platforms. He has written and produced television and film projects, and soon to be releasing a relationship app to help couples communicate more effectively.

Ivory grew up on the outskirts of Philadelphia, Pa. in a small town called Bristol. After high school, Ivory received a basketball scholarship that took him to Northern California where he ultimately received his bachelor's degree in psychology.

He currently resides in Los Angeles where he lives with his three amazing daughters and awesome dog, Rogee.

Made in the USA
San Bernardino, CA
24 July 2020

75573603R00075